T0198396

Organs
and
Organisms

An Explanation of Everything

Written and Illustrated by

Les Braunstein

Copyright © 2021 Les Braunstein.

All rights reserved. No part of this book may be used or reproduced by any means, graphic, electronic, or mechanical, including photocopying, recording, taping or by any information storage retrieval system without the written permission of the author except in the case of brief quotations embodied in critical articles and reviews.

This book is a work of non-fiction. Unless otherwise noted, the author and the publisher make no explicit guarantees as to the accuracy of the information contained in this book and in some cases, names of people and places have been altered to protect their privacy.

Archway Publishing books may be ordered through booksellers or by contacting:

Archway Publishing
1663 Liberty Drive
Bloomington, IN 47403
www.archwaypublishing.com
844-669-3957

Because of the dynamic nature of the Internet, any web addresses or links contained in this book may have changed since publication and may no longer be valid. The views expressed in this work are solely those of the author and do not necessarily reflect the views of the publisher, and the publisher hereby disclaims any responsibility for them.

Any people depicted in stock imagery provided by Getty Images are models, and such images are being used for illustrative purposes only.
Certain stock imagery © Getty Images.

ISBN: 978-1-6657-0847-0 (sc)
ISBN: 978-1-6657-0848-7 (e)

Print information available on the last page.

Archway Publishing rev. date: 9/3/2021

Chapter 1

(Where-in the author reveals a straight fact)

Since the human began to talk it has had lots of ideas about what it was. It looked at the world working all around magically and perfectly. The sun appeared and disappeared. The weather grew warm, then cold, then warm again. There were plants and animals for food and clothes. There was the warm excitement of joining with another human. Smells, tastes, pain, everything. And order, so much order. Everything working. Everything right. So much to wonder at. So much to take for granted. So much to fear.

The human looked at the animals. Some were stronger. Some were faster. But the human survived by the power of its very good brain and one by one established power over the quicker and stronger animals, caused plants to grow where it wished, held back the cold with fire and shelter, and began to think.

"What am I?" it thought. I don't make the sun rise and fall. Something must be above me. I have beaten the animals, they must be below me. "And after all," it reasoned (as it began to reason) "I can reason!, and that makes me sparklingly different from all I find around. It must be that the thing above me has placed me above the beasts - Master of the Earth. I am something great and terrible. Not a god, of course, but god-like above all else.

My will be done."

The human forgot it couldn't easily swing from tree to tree - or jump 5 times its height like a cat - or fly like a bird. It didn't see that the order came from everything taking its place. Playing its part.

So the human - the planet's greatest brain - closed its eye and began to grow.

Much, much, much, much later when the human was no longer quite so sure there was any power above, "Earth, Moon, rain, stars all seem quite natural," it observed, certain humans came up with the idea that Man had erupted from the animals. Well, most humans didn't like that idea, but it slowly began to be believed. Still the human clung to its superiority - it had erupted out from and above the animals

"What is it that separates us from the animals?" the human is fond of asking.

Here is the answer.

Nothing.

You're an animal.

Chapter 2

Organisms and organs

An organism is a unit of life. It is a total living structure
going through its day, feeding and reproducing, doing
all the operations it needs to survive. To better
understand this I will draw 3 organisms

1 a plant organism 2 an animal organism 3 a thing that looks very
much like mold on an orange
but is really a planetary
system organism

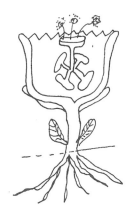  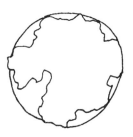

All organisms are systems, that is, different parts of the organism fulfill different functions which are necessary for the organism's survival.

Thus in the plant organism:

Pollen on the Stamen (male part)

The stamens and pistols are hard at work reproducing

Sticky pistols (female part)

while the roots are hard at work hunting up water

Any entire part of that system - like the root or the female part is an organ.

Chapter 3

Where we learn that one man's organism, is another man's organ.

An organism can also be viewed as an organ of a larger organism.

To illustrate this fact I will use an animal organism- in this case a human, although it is always sensible to remember that we might as well be talking about chipmunks. All the same.

Here we have a human, in this case a male. There is no denying that he is an organism. If he were captured by extraterrestrials from Alpha Centauri and brought back to their star system, he would be poked and prodded and discussed as this strange organism from Earth.

However, after 70 or 80 years he would die. But why? Why do organisms die? Don't their organs function well enough? Or is this only the death of an organ?

This particular living structure is not complete. It cannot reproduce itself without the female counterpart. It plays the same role as the male part of the flower. When an organism reproduces it does not create a new organism. It extends itself by another generation - another link in the chain. There were parts before, there will be parts after. All connected All the same organism.

to make this clear:

When you emerged from your mother you were connected by a tube that was grown by your mother just as she grew you. You and she were attached, one piece of living thing. This cord had to be cut (or chewed if that was your sort of mother). It would have fallen away anyway but suppose it had remained, we would see:

Now if you were in a helicopter and looked down and saw all this coming down the road, you would probably say "Look. there's some weird organism creeping along the ground." Because this is definitely an organism. Just like a plant with many blossoms.

Now remove all the cords (for convenience, mobility, etc.) and each piece is no less part of the organism. (Remember, they'll need each other again to reproduce.)

It is the nature of an animal organism that the individual parts are unconnected physically, although they are still part of the inter dependent system. Each loose part is called an individual.

In the animal organism that we have been discussing there are two sorts of individuals - male individuals and female individuals.

Male individuals are like the fertilizing powders of the plant or like the fingers of your left hand. They are the male organs of the one human organism. Individual organs but the same organism. Sexually they can be interchanged. all programed to produce another human individual. All the same which is why, although they can be interestingly different, basically they all act the same.

Female individuals are like plant's seed cups or like the fingers on your right hand. They are the female organs of the one human organism. Individual organs but the same organism. Sexually they can be interchanged. They are like the seed cups of the plant. All programed to produce another human, all the same which is why a woman you meet can suddenly remind you of your mother or your sister or a woman you knew a long time ago.

Neither male nor female individuals are more important than the other kind. Without each other they can't reproduce, and without reproducing the organism will die.

Humanity - the total human organism hasn't died yet (unlike the Brontosaurus organism.) Only individuals finish their jobs and disappear like blossoms falling off an apple tree -

All replaced.

All all right.

All for the best.

Chapter 4

Races

If you take three offspring from the same plant and put one in the desert, one in a forest, and one on a mountain, they will survive by developing characteristics necessary for their new environments. After a great number of generations the desert plants might have leathery skin to protect against too much sun and long roots to hunt for water. The forest plants might have broad leaves to catch whatever sunlight filters through the trees. While the mountain plants might look the same because they had no reason to change.

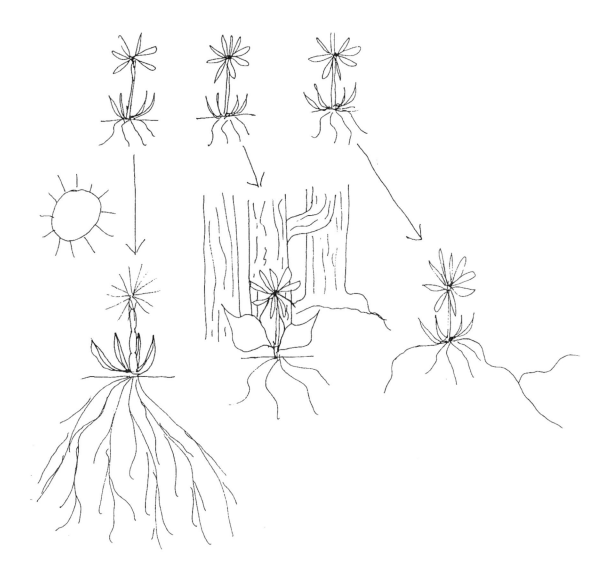

This is why there are black Africans and pale Scandinavians and Asians and all the rest. Since originally they came from the same organism they will reproduce together quite well.

And mixing keeps an organism healthy.

Chapter 5

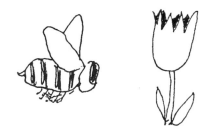

Plant - Animal Organisms

Some plants don't depend on pollen falling or being carried by the wind to the seed. A bee lands there looking for sweet flower nectar to make honey. He gets pollen on his feet and then flies off and lands on another flower where the pollen touches a seed.

If you were to draw the reproductive cycle of that flower you would have to include the bee. If you were to draw the way the bee produces its honey food, you would have to include the flower.

They are 2 organisms. And each is an organ in the one bigger organism.

Chapter 6

Or meanwhile back at the moldy orange or where the everything comes in.

Even humanity isn't complete. like the human individual on Alpha Centauri, it can not survive without the other organisms that supply it with food - replenish its air - and do all the rest. Organisms like all the other animals and all the plants that along with humanity are the organs of the one large organism that lives here on Earth.

An apple tree stands feeding on soil rich in minerals left there by the droppings and bones of animals. In the spring its apple blossoms bloom and are pollenated by the feet of bumble bees. In the summer sun its leaves give off oxygen for the animals to breathe. In the fall it wraps all its sugar-food around its seeds and drops them - apples - to the ground. One is eaten by the birds and one is carried off by a squirrel - half eaten- then buried and forgotten - where after a winter's wait the seed feeds on the animal rich soil - and continues.

It wasn't just chance brought the bee to the tree. Each has its function. Each supports the whole. Each is an organ in the planetary organism. Each is still an organism, going about its business. And each fulfills its function in the organism - Earth.

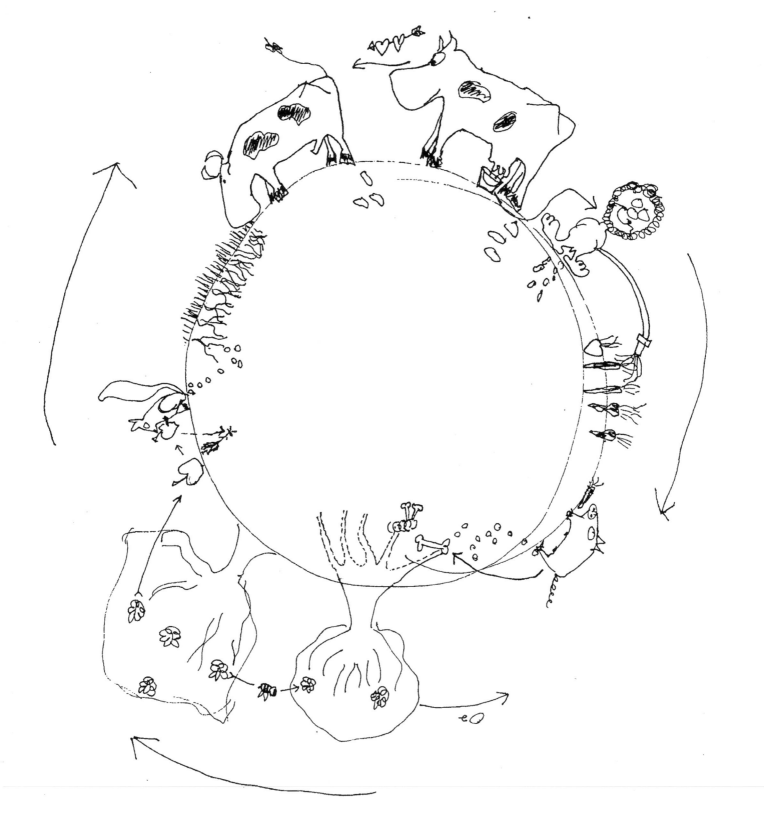

Chapter 7

What's going on?

You were born at an exciting time. It is what's known as a cusp, which means a time of great change - the ending of one period and the beginning of another. Many human individuals will tell you that this time is just like all other times but this is not so, and here is why.

In the past when a human learned something (fire hurts, some berries can be eaten, some can't) it could pass that knowledge on to other humans. Other humans in its tribe or village. As humans began to roam they could pass ideas from town to town, tribe to tribe, even country to country. An idea from the brain of one human could be built upon by the brain of another.

When the human began to write things down (not so very long ago) there was suddenly a much greater opportunity for humans to build ideas upon other human ideas.

Today ideas flash through the air with the speed of light - radio, television, the telephone and now the internet pass ideas around the world through satellites and cables so that one human idea can join with others anywhere on the globe. Now your tribe includes humans everywhere. Your brain and theirs, every brain on the planet can be joined for the first time into a great

planetary brain.

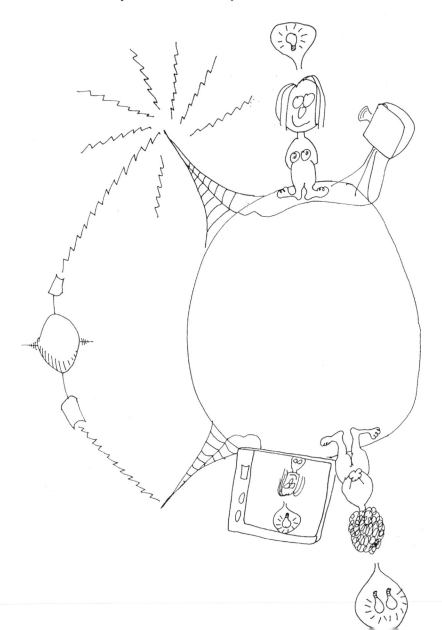

The human has migrated around the world from where the sun rises in Asia, across, Africa, Europe and the Americas - to where it drops beyond the California seas. The human organism has reached the ocean islands and crossed the snowy polar reaches. It has descended into the waters and ascended into the clouds. It has touched where it began and it finally sees that the land is not endless - the forests can all be counted - the buffalo can all be killed - the world is not endless. Our home is a ball. A planet. A sphere hung lightly in space......

......and not only that, but humans, astronauts, for the very first time - have leaped off the Earth - and looked back and we see that we are all Earthlings - Terrestrials - animals of the Earth

And because we know all that the most amazing thing of all has happened........

THE HUMAN HAS OPENED ITS EYE.

Chapter 8

What the human sees

The human has been thrashing about with its eye closed for a very long time - so it comes as no surprise - now that its open - that humanity (with its very powerful brain) sees it has made quite a mess. It discovered that it had not been noticing that it was an organ in a big planet wide organism - or even that each human was connected to all the others.

These are some things that we see:

We see that the humans before us had been consuming the other organs - plant and animal - at a great rate. Partly because they thought they were the only important organism - and partly because they had not been thinking about the world as a globe and so they thought there would always be more.

We see that the humans before us had not been noticing that the other individuals, plant and animal - were not only necessary but were busy going on with their own lives and could feel. So, they had been killing other animals just for fun, and chopping down whole forests -throwing garbage into the ocean and even destroying other humans in big and painful ways.

And we see that the human organism is growing to dangerous size. Just so we can really understand this very great problem, I will tell you about rats. If you put some rat individuals in a cage and give them food and water, there will soon be a lot more. In fact they will reproduce until it gets very crowded in the cage. Before long there will be so many rats in the cage that their droppings and other wastes will begin to get into their food and water. Then disease will begin and they will begin to fight. In the end they will all be dead. And that kind of population problem, could occur to humans in our cage - the Earth- during your lifetime. In fact - look at our weather, our waters, and our air - it has begun.

Now every organism when faced with danger or great need brings forth or develops mechanisms to protect and heal itself. Your blood produces antibodies to fight disease in your system. The desert plant grew leathery skin through mutation. Humanity, and indeed the entire planetary organism is facing great danger. And just now, at this very moment, the Earth is developing a powerful defense mechanism to protect its life.

And that mechanism is you.

You are the open-eyed human
You see that the Earth is a ball of a certain limited size.
That it's possible to sicken and even destroy
the life system on it.

You see it and you yourself personally cannot order the destruction of whole forests. You cannot open a factory that pours poison into the skies. You can no longer want to kill or waste or cause pain or have a ridiculous number of children or simply thrash about blindly and make a mess.

And not because I pass a law or make a rule but because each human individual is doing what it sees it should. Not because it's being told to- but because each of us can feel whatever pain we give to the rest of the organism. And each of us sees that

The better you live

the better your life.

And one by one we return to our natural roles as animals in the system. Animals who specialize in thinking because of our open eye and our very good brain.

Epilogue

Since the human began to talk it has had a lot of ideas about what it was. And that was the problem. Its ideas, its myths covered the answer, the simple answer, that lay on the ground, flew in the air, swam in the seas and danced all around -

We are the birds, the trees, the deer, the humen, the fish
We are all of it
And we live or die
Together

We are the life, the eruption of matter into organized force. We are a turning of the universe. We are the eaters of suns, the dancers of space, the brothers of rock, the sisters of light. We are the Terrestrial organism. A life of the universe.

There are millions of suns. Uncountable billions. They do the chemical dance - breathe heat and light into the spatial wait.

And we are the life. And we are the brain. The horses, the moles, the corn and the grass. We are the hum - the glow of the Earth.

We are Terrestria
an organ of the universe.

a song in the stars.

The choice is yours
the change is in you

Live Life

Remember your body

Feel the power - your animal power

Enjoy it all

Know what you do.

Do what you will.

Be Free

Get to the country and feel the world.

Run in a forest.

run like a beast

Scream like an animal

Laugh like a bird

Reach for you partners,

Animal, Vegetable, and Human partners

Touch them, feel them, roll and dive

eat

smell

see

taste

and live, you animal

Live!

27

Printed in the United States
by Baker & Taylor Publisher Services